Digital Downpour
The Mindful Gamer's Guide

Table of Contents

Chapter 1. Introduction

Just like a refreshing downpour revives the earth, the world of digital gaming can invigorate our minds. Yet, without a mindful guide, the deluge of digital content can be overwhelming. Welcome to our Special Report, "Digital Downpour: The Mindful Gamer's Guide". This comprehensive report is your key to navigating the ever-evolving gaming industry, enhancing your gaming experience and fostering healthy habits. Delve into exclusive interviews with leading game developers, innovative gaming strategies, and expert advice on maintaining a balance between the virtual and the real world. This report is not just about winning the game; it's about winning at life through the lens of a gamer! Let this Special Report be your guiding light in the digital downpour, illuminating a path that perfectly blends entertainment with mindfulness. Be prepared to enter a new stage of your gaming journey, becoming a mindful player in this vast digital realm!

Chapter 2. Unraveling the Digital Downpour: An Overview

In the riveting world of digital gaming, every innovation is akin to a cascading shower, pouring new possibilities into the universe of play. As in a heavy downpour, the sheer volume of changes, advancements, and opportunities can at times feel overpowering. To successfully navigate this landscape, it's essential to understand its contours, including the trends shaping its growth and the multifaceted impacts of digital gaming on our lives.

2.1. The Landscape of Digital Gaming

Digital gaming's transformative journey started with straightforward 8-bit games and has evolved to encompass intricate, hyper-realistic environments powered by sophisticated artificial intelligence (AI) and augmented reality (AR) technologies. The pace of change is extraordinary. Every year, game developers push boundaries and recalibrate expectations by delivering experiences that were unimaginable a decade ago.

From the singular world of 'Pong' to multiple realms in 'World of Warcraft', digital gaming's expansive landscape now spans various platforms - PC, console, mobile, and cloud gaming. New genres have emerged, targeting wildly different demographics and integrating captivating narratives, strategic gameplay, and high-quality graphics that charm casual and hardcore gamers alike. Furthermore, the rise of eSports has catapulted digital gaming onto a global stage, creating a vibrant professional league where expert gamers compete for recognition and rewards.

2.2. The Players: Diversity and Growth

The digital gaming community's profile has evolved dramatically over the years. Once stereotyped as lone teenagers relegated to darkened rooms, today's gamers are an immensely diverse crowd, incorporating different ages, genders, and geographical locations. The rise of mobile gaming has catalyzed this transformation, making games more accessible to a broader audience.

In the heart of this digital gaming surge are millennials and Gen Z, captivated by the vibrant visuals, engaging narratives, and opportunities for social interaction. Yet, they're not the entirety. Increasingly, older adults are embracing digital games for cognitive stimulation, stress relief, and sheer entertainment. The inclusion of women gamers has also been a landmark change, with females representing nearly half of the global gamer population.

2.3. The Psychological Impact of Digital Games

Recent research reveals that digital gaming, often maligned for promoting sedentary behavior and antisocial tendencies, can have positive psychological impacts. Contrary to the notion that gaming isolates individuals, many games promote social interaction, teamwork, and collaborative problem-solving. Online games provide a platform for community-building, allowing individuals to form friendships and networks based on mutual interests.

Beyond the social benefits, digital games can also significantly boost cognitive abilities. Fast-paced games necessitate quick decision-making, enhancing gamers' reflexes and strategic thinking. Puzzle-oriented games improve problem-solving skills, while immersive games with complex narratives can boost memory and attention span.

Digital games have found therapeutic applications, too. They've been used to treat conditions like ADHD and dyslexia and to enhance physical therapy outcomes. Moreover, digital games have played a key role in fostering resilience during challenging times. Amid the Covid-19 pandemic, games provided individuals with an outlet for relaxation and social connection while physical distancing.

However, as with any powerful tool, gaming entails risks when misused. Excessive gaming can lead to unhealthy lifestyle habits and even addiction. Moreover, the anonymity of online platforms sometimes fosters harassment or bullying.

2.4. Healthier Gaming Habits: Balancing the Real and Virtual

Finding balance in digital gaming is vital to ensure its benefits are harnesses while mitigating potential risks. In the quest for equilibrium, establishing physical boundaries is crucial. For example, regular breaks from gaming can allow rest for the eyes and body.

On the psychological front, fostering a positive community is incredibly beneficial. This not only enhances the enjoyment of the game but also safeguards against negative encounters online. Additionally, diversifying one's leisure activities can provide a well-rounded experience, preventing overreliance on gaming for entertainment or stress relief.

In the digital age, parental guidance has never been more critical. By understanding the games their children play and setting reasonable time limits, parents can guide their children through the digital gaming realm.

2.5. Navigating the Future of Digital Gaming

As the digital gaming industry continues to evolve, being a mindful gamer will be more important than ever. Emerging trends like VR, AR, and AI will make the gaming experience increasingly immersive. Blockchain technology could revolutionize gaming economies, and the continued rise of eSports will offer more opportunities for gamers to turn their passion into a profession.

While these advancements will undoubtedly enhance the gaming experience, they will also introduce new challenges. It's essential to develop strategies for managing these impacts, fostering healthy gaming habits, and maintaining balance between the virtual and the real world.

Indeed, the digital downpour in gaming can be overwhelming—but it also brings tremendous possibilities. By understanding the changing landscape of gaming and its impact on players, we can navigate the deluge with confidence and transform it into a force for entertainment, education, and mental agility. Whether you're a casual player, a gaming enthusiast, or a parent guiding your child through the gaming world, understanding this landscape can help ensure a fulfilling and balanced gaming experience.

Chapter 3. The Mindful Gamer: Redefining the Game

Gaming, despite being a popular form of entertainment, often suffers from a variety of stereotypes and myths. To name just a few, pervasive beliefs include that gaming promotes aggression, social isolation, or addictive behaviors. Yet, a new breed of mindful gamers is emerging, tearing down these stereotypes and reshaping the contours of the gaming landscape. This chapter is an in-depth exploration of the concept of the mindful gamer, examining how mindfulness can elevate the gaming experience, foster healthier habits, and bring about a more thoughtful and engaged mode of game interaction.

3.1. Defining the Mindful Gamer

The term "mindful" comes from the practice of mindfulness, a form of meditation rooted in Buddhist tradition, now firmly established within Western psychology due to its proven therapeutic benefits. Mindfulness is about being wholly present in the moment, attentive of one's thoughts, emotions, sensations, and surroundings without any judgment. This heightened awareness of the self and its relation to the immediate environment nurtures emotional regulation, stress management, and cognitive flexibility.

A mindful gamer, then, is one who brings this level of attentiveness to their gaming experience. Mindful gamers are actively conscious of their actions, reactions, and emotions as they navigate through their gaming world. Instead of being absorbed in a cycle of compulsive play and high arousal, they seek to find an equilibrium between excitement and relaxation, challenge and resilience, escapism and reality.

They are also aware of the implications and effects of their gaming habits on their personal health and social interactions. They understand the ways in which their gaming preferences and practices may reflect their personality traits or psychological states, offering them insights not just about their in-game character, but about their character in the larger game of life.

3.2. From Addictive to Meditative: The Cultural Transformation

Gone are the days when gaming was just a time-sink, a social taboo, or an addictive vice. The collective cultural notion about gaming has been transforming at a fast pace. And at the heart of this change are the mindful gamers themselves.

Becoming a mindful gamer isn't just about rehabilitation from damaging gaming habits or addiction. It is a holistic lifestyle choice that encourages positive mental health, deeper self-understanding and social bonding through shared gaming experiences. A game then is not just a game, but a tool for self-improvement, exploration, and connection. The narrative is slowly changing from the perceived negativity of "Gaming Addiction" to the positivity of "Gaming Meditation."

Today's mindful gamers are getting rid of the guilt and stigma traditionally associated with gaming. They facilitate discussions around gaming's impact on mental health and productivity, leading the cultural shift from blame and prohibition to understanding and inclusion.

3.3. Gaming as a Mindful Practice

Gaming can be a form of meditative practice that fosters mindfulness skills. Below are ways that gaming aligns with mindfulness:

- Presence: Games demand our full attention. They help us practice being present in the moment, blocking out distractions. This mirrors the mindfulness practice of anchoring our attention to an object, sound, or movement.

- Flow: A concept introduced by psychologist Mihaly Csikszentmihalyi, flow is a state of intense focus and optimal experience where time seems to stand still. For gamers, these moments of flow can lead to heightened awareness and a sense of fulfillment.

- Emotional Regulation: Games evoke a range of emotions, from joy to frustration. They offer a safe environment to explore and manage these feelings, fostering emotional intelligence.

- Social Connection: Multiplayer games cultivate empathy, teamwork, and connection with diverse individuals across the globe.

- Recognition: Games reward progress and celebrate achievements. These micro-victories promote self-confidence and positive mental health.

However, gamers need to play responsibly and in moderation. Just as excessive exercise can lead to injuries, obsessive gaming can lead to addiction, anxiety, and other related health issues. Hence, balance is crucial in achieving a mindful gaming experience.

3.4. Reinventing Gaming Habits for Mindfulness

A mindful gamer forms habits that optimize the gaming experience while minimizing potential harm. Here are some practical tips to realign gaming habits with mindfulness:

1. Regulate Playtime: Define healthy boundaries for playing time to avoid over-indulgence. The key is moderation.

2. Healthy Gaming Environment: Keep your gaming environment

clean, cozy and ergonomic to minimize physical stress.

3. Breaks and Exercise: Incorporating regular breaks and physical activities during gaming sessions can prevent stiffness, ensure better circulation, and keep the mind fresh.

4. Socialize: Participate in multi-player games or gaming communities to share experiences and broaden your perspective.

5. Conscious Consuming: Be selective of the content you choose to play, as games can influence your emotional and mental state.

6. Reflective Gameplay: Regularly introspect your emotional state during and after gameplay. It promotes emotional understanding and control.

7. Gaming Journal: Maintain a gaming journal to record thoughts, feelings, and discoveries. This can provide profound insights about both your gaming and real-life experiences.

Incorporating mindfulness into gaming can transform the casual gamer into the mindful gamer: attuned, balanced, and fully engaged. And as the gaming world continues to advance, offering increasingly immersive and innovative experiences, the mindfulness practice within gaming will further offer a path to personal growth, mental health balance, and an enriched human connection.

At the crux of this change is the mindful gamer who, just as a Zen master does, is redefining the game not through mastery skills, aggression or high scores but through a serene mind, a conscious presence and a compassionate heart.

Chapter 4. Becoming a Digital Nomad: Navigating the Gaming Landscape

The digital landscape can be as vast and confusing as a new city or continent to a novice traveler. Learning to navigate this terrain is an essential part of becoming a successful and balanced digital nomad. This guide aims to take you through a step-by-step journey, covering all the essential aspects of becoming a master gamer while maintaining a healthy balance between the virtual and physical world.

4.1. Understanding the Gaming Landscape

The world of gaming is vast, encompassing multiple genres and platforms. There are role-playing games (RPGs), first-person shooters (FPS), strategy games, simulation games, and more, each with its unique attributes and appeal. On the platform side, you have consoles such as Xbox and PlayStation, computer games, and mobile gaming. It's important to identify the genre and platform that best suits your interests, skills, and lifestyle.

Beginners often start with easily accessible mobile games or popular big-budget console games to immerse themselves in the gaming landscape. As your skills and interests evolve, exploring different games and platforms becomes an organic process. It's crucial to understand that there's no 'one-size-fits-all' in gaming. What works for someone might not work for you, and that's perfectly fine.

4.2. Acquiring the Necessary Skills

Just like learning a musical instrument or a new sport, gaming involves acquiring skills over time. Patience and persistence are vital, particularly when dealing with complex games that include multiple levels, intricate narratives, or competitive multiplayer scenarios.

While each game requires a certain set of unique skills, some common abilities cut across the gaming sphere. These include strategic thinking, response speed, task management, and teamwork, especially relevant in multiplayer games where you collaborate with other players toward a common objective.

There's a common misconception that gaming is merely an act of mindless indulgence. However, serious gaming can improve various cognitive abilities such as multitasking, problem-solving, and hand-eye coordination, which prove useful outside the gaming sphere, making this digital nomad journey an enriching one.

4.3. Building a Gaming Library

One of the most delightful aspects of being a gamer is building your own gaming library. This doesn't mean acquiring every new game that hits the market. True gamers often have carefully curated collections of games that hold some personal significance, whether it's an engrossing storyline, challenging gameplay, or simply the nostalgic value of a childhood favorite.

Take time to research before purchasing a game. Read reviews, watch gameplay videos, and perhaps try a demonstration if available. Consider how much time you're willing to invest in the game, as some titles require hundreds of hours to complete thoroughly.

Remember, quality trumps quantity when it comes to building a meaningful gaming library.

4.4. Balancing Gaming with Real Life

While gaming can be an entertaining and enlivening adventure, it's essential to strike a balance between the virtual and real world. Gaming should never feel like an escape from reality but rather a complement to your life, enhancing your experiences rather than replacing them.

Ensure your gaming habits don't interfere with your personal or professional obligations. Regular breaks are essential, both during gaming sessions and between them. Incorporate physical activity into your daily routine, maintaining a healthy lifestyle that supports your gaming hobby.

Mindful gaming also involves being aware of the content you're engaging with. Some games might include violent or sensitive themes that could affect your mental health. Ensure that your gaming experience is a positive one, contributing to your overall wellbeing.

4.5. Joining the Gaming Community

Gaming is not an isolated affair. Over the years, a vibrant and diverse community has grown around gaming, connected by a shared enthusiasm for the virtual world. Joining gaming communities, both online and offline, can enrich your gaming experience significantly.

Whether it's a forum dedicated to a particular game where you can share strategies, a local gaming club, or even international game conventions, these platforms offer opportunities to learn, exchange ideas, and form friendships. Remember, respectful communication and mutual respect are the foundations of a healthy community experience.

4.6. Gaming and Mindfulness

In modern conversations around mental health, the concept of mindfulness repeatedly emerges as a crucial element. Mindfulness means being present in the current moment, fully engaged and aware of your experiences. Contrary to typical assumptions, gaming can contribute to mindfulness.

The immersive nature of gaming means players often need to be fully aware of the game's mechanics, narratives, and player dynamics. Engaged gaming can, therefore, enhance your ability to concentrate and immerse yourself fully in tasks outside the gaming world too.

The key lies in viewing gaming not as a mindless hobby but as an active engagement with a dynamic and enticing digital landscape. As you embrace this journey, the world of gaming becomes a realm of strategic decision-making, narrative exploration, aesthetic appreciation, and cognitive challenge.

Embrace the rain of this digital downpour. Become the digital nomad who navigates the gaming landscape effortlessly, armed with wisdom accumulated from a lifetime of explorations. This is as much a journey of self-discovery and personal growth as it is about high scores and victorious battles. Let this guide lead you towards the watershed moment of your gaming journey, where entertainment and mindfulness converge. This is not just about winning the game; it's about winning at life, through the lens of a gamer.

Chapter 5. Behind the Screens: Interviews with the Creators

From the conceptualization to the culmination of a video game, an array of creative geniuses spin their magic behind the screens. These creators are illustrators, designers, developers, and writers working cohesively to offer gamers an immersive world of digital possibility. Their insights on the gaming industry, their creation, and the ways they envisage the future of gaming can illuminate a myriad of aspects for a mindful gamer.

5.1. Meeting the Developer: Journey towards Game Creation

Perhaps, the most significant part of game development is the idea that sparks the process. An interview with Esther Stuart, a seasoned game developer and the brain behind the successful multiplayer online game "Cosmic Conquest", revealed the intricacies involved in the initial phases of game development.

"The kernel of an idea can pop up from anywhere—the lyrics of a song, a vivid dream, or even the memory of a childhood game. The trick is to detect that spark and then nurture it into a full-fledged concept," she stated. Her revolutionary game, Cosmic Conquest, began one day when she was gazing at the stars, contemplating the mysteries of the universe, and the endless possibilities that lay in there. *"When I brought this celestial concept to the team, it was surreal—just a vague boundary that needed refining through brainstorming sessions, countless cups of coffee, and a common belief in the idea,"* Esther explained.

5.2. Character Development: Crafting Identities

Gary Reynolds, known for inventing extraordinary characters like Tyara, the friendly fire-breathing dragon, enlightened us about character development.

"Developing characters is like being a demigod. You instill life into non-living entities, crafting their stories and defining their personalities. You're giving them power to interact with players," Reynolds shared. For Tyara, he drew inspiration from his daughter's favorite plush toy, a stuffed dragon. *"I wanted to make a non-threatening but funny, lovable character for kids to interact with. Tyara's personality was a reflection of my daughter's liveliness."* It was a beautiful blend of creativity, reality, and deep understanding of target audiences that led to Tyara's immense popularity.

5.3. World-Building: Constructing Realms and Reality

World-building is integral to gaming, and who better to shed light on it than Ivana McPherson, renowned for her exceptional work on "Underwater Odyssey". Ivana described world-building as *"an articulation of the game developer's imagination put in a perceivable form for the gamer's adventures."* For the deep-sea world of "Underwater Odyssey", the team strived to emulate real-life marine architecture and hypothesized underwater habitats. Precision in design and dedication to authenticity made the game a visual treat in addition to an engaging play.

5.4. Story Writing: Weaving the Narrative Web

Storytelling is an art, and in the gaming universe, it plays a pivotal role in engaging players. Narrative mastermind Linus Ortega, renowned for his best-selling game "Mystic Quest", unraveled the secret thread of game storytelling. According to Linus, *"A good story gives a profound purpose to the game. It's like the North Star guiding players in their digital journey."*

5.5. Game Mechanics: The Final Touch

Once the conceptual groundwork is laid – characters are created, worlds built and stories are written – it's time for a crucial phase in game development, i.e., designing the game mechanics. Cecil Boyd, a wizard in implementing mechanics, detailed its significance. *"Game mechanics are the spinal cord of a video game. They define how a player interacts with the game world, how the game responds, and ultimately shapes the player's experience,"* said Cecil.

Behind these screens, ideas come to life, ready to be explored, enjoyed and learned from. These creators' insights underline the essence of being a mindful gamer – respecting the effort put into a game, appreciating the attention to detail, and the ability to lose oneself in the plot but still maintain a balanced perspective on reality. They reinforce the idea that video games are not merely diversions but are artistic expressions and platforms for storytelling that can impact our minds, teaching lessons, imparting values, and provoking thoughts in ways that spill over into our real lives.

Chapter 6. Game On: Strategies for the New Age Gamer

In a world that sees constant technological evolution and innovation, the landscape of digital gaming continues to adapt and transform. With the rapid growth of this industry, new strategic approaches to gameplay are emerging. Whether you're a hardened veteran or a novice at the console, here are some unique gaming strategies to enhance your experiences in this new gaming age.

6.1. Approach Each Game as a New Learning Experience

Just as life never stops teaching, gaming never stops offering new mechanics and narratives. Treat every new game as a fresh opportunity to acquire knowledge. No matter how skilled you are, every game requires a fresh understanding of its unique mechanisms and idiosyncrasies. Study the game closely before diving into its narrative. Get to know level layouts, NPC behavior patterns, and the strengths and weaknesses of enemies. Remember, intentional practice and patience will empower your gameplay.

6.2. Mastering Controls

In any game, controls are the bridge between the player and the virtual world. While many games share similar control schemes, each game can vary subtly or drastically. Delve into the game's control settings and take the time to adapt to it. In many cases, games offer control customization options. Utilize these to tailor controls in a way that's most comfortable for you. A great gamer is the one who has mastered the nerves of their avatar, moving them around as an extension of themselves.

6.3. Patience, Persistence and Strategy

Gaming is not merely about action; it's a lot about precision and strategy. Consider games like chess or poker. The same strategic thinking and patience can often apply to the fast-paced, high-stakes world of digital gaming. Use patience and a carefully thought-out approach to leverage your position in the game. Slow and steady can often win the race in gaming, just as in life.

6.4. Embrace Multiplayer Dynamics

Multiplayer gaming isn't just about competition; it's about cooperation, too. Many games are built on the ethos of community and teamwork. Participating in these can be a uniquely rewarding experience. Engage in collaborative problem-solving, share strategies, and enhance your social skills in the process. Regardless of the game genre, multiplayer interactions can be a rich source of learning and enjoyment.

6.5. Dealing with Ingame Economy

Understanding the in-game economy is integral to advancing in many games. Whether it consists of gold coins, virtual cash, or mystical gems, mastering the art of managing, spending and investing these resources is crucial. This aspect often reflects principles found in the real-world economy, promoting wise spending, thoughtful investment, and management.

6.6. Adaptability: Key to Survival

Remember that the only constant in life is change. This holds true in digital gaming where developers introduce updates, patches and expansions to keep the gameplay fresh and engaging. Ensure you always adapt to new gameplay elements, mechanics, and rule changes. Let adaptability be your strength in each gaming endeavor.

6.7. Gaming Ethics and Fair Play

While succeeding in a game is important, maintaining ethics and fair play should always be prioritized. Cheating, grieving, or bullying other players can lead to a toxic gaming experience for everyone involved. Uplift the digital community with your presence by promoting good conduct for a healthier gaming environment.

In an ever-evolving industry, staying fresh and driven in your approach to gaming can maximize your experience. Through each hard-fought battle, tricky puzzle, and in-game dialogue, you'll refine key skills transferrable to real-life situations. These are the strategies for the new age gamer: a mindful, respectful, and engaged participant in the digital downpour. As you switch on your consoles and computers, remember to immerse and enrich yourself, not just in gameplay, but in life itself. Ensure your gaming journey, under the rain of digital downpour, is one marked with growth, creativity, and delight!

Chapter 7. Virtual vs. Reality: Striking a Balance

In the past couple of decades, the gaming industry has drastically morphed into an immersive landscape, where the elements of reality and fantasy intertwine to allure players into an enchanting virtual world. Amidst the mesmerizing visuals and plotlines, striking a balance between the virtual and real world might seem challenging at times. However, understanding the impact of digital gaming on daily life, setting realistic limits, and implementing strategies promoting responsible gaming habits could help you walk this tightrope proficiently.

7.1. Understanding the Impact

One cannot strike a balance without understanding the weight at both ends of the scale. In this instance, it is crucial to comprehend how digital gaming affects your daily life. Gaming is not inherently detrimental. In fact, many studies showcase its benefits, such as improved hand-eye coordination, problem-solving abilities, and stress relief.

However, excessive gaming can lead to dependence, negatively impacting your physical health, relationships, and career. Signs of extreme gaming include neglected duties, increased isolation, obsessive game-related thoughts, and poor physical health due to a sedentary lifestyle. Striking a balance begins with acknowledging the impact your gaming habits have on your life.

7.2. Setting Realistic Limits

Striking a balance does not mean you have to give up gaming; it's about gaming responsibly. Knowing your standards and setting realistic boundaries can help achieve this balance.

Start by assessing the amount of time you spend gaming. How many hours per week are spent in front of the screen? Are there times when you neglect family, work, or self-care to play games? Use these reflections to determine a daily or weekly limit for gaming that fits into your life, without encroaching on your obligations.

There are various tools available to assist you in this, such as mobile apps and gaming console settings, which have features to limit screen time actively.

7.3. The Art of Time Management

While setting limits is essential, effectively managing your time within those constraints is equally important. Determine which periods are most suitable for gaming, considering your professional and personal obligations. Additionally, prioritize responsibilities such as work, fitness, and family time before indulging in your gaming sessions.

Use a schedule or a planner to organize your day. A well-structured day can help maintain a healthy lifestyle and ensure that the elements of leisure, like gaming, do not overpower your daily functioning.

7.4. Gaming and Health

While immersing oneself in a digital world can be exciting, it's crucial not to neglect physical health. Prolonged gaming sessions can lead to a sedentary lifestyle, which can increase the risk of obesity, heart disease, and other health issues.

Ensure to take regular breaks during gaming to stretch, hydrate, and rest your eyes. Incorporate a daily fitness routine to counterbalance the extended periods of immobility associated with gaming. Remember that a healthier body can lead to a better gaming experience.

7.5. Nurturing Real-Life Relationships

Gaming can be socially rewarding, introducing you to fellow gamers from various walks of life. However, your real-life relationships should not suffer because of your gaming habits. Allocate sufficient time to interact with family and friends offline.

Exploring other shared hobbies or activities outside of gaming can strengthen your relationships and provide a more rounded social experience.

7.6. Seeking Professional Help

If you feel that gaming is taking over your life, causing significant discomfort, it may be prudent to seek professional help. Therapists and counselors trained in dealing with gaming addiction can provide the support and tools needed to curb excessive gaming and regain control over your life.

7.7. Conclusion

Striking a balance between gaming and reality is a dynamic process that requires ongoing attention and adjustments. It's about making conscious choices that work for you, allowing you to maximize the benefits and joy that gaming offers while ensuring a healthy, fulfilling real-life existence. After all, as the sayings go, 'Life is more fun if you play games,' but 'game over' should never mean 'life over.'

Chapter 8. The Healthful Player: Tips for Physical and Mental Well-being

Gaming offers a captivating world where we can become knights, astronauts, adventurers, or virtually anything we can imagine. Yet, as alluring as these landscapes can be, it is vital to remain grounded in reality, safeguarding our physical and mental wellbeing. This segment delves into the various facets of a gamer's life, underscoring the importance of creating habits that ensure good health and a mindful gaming experience.

8.1. Gaming and Physical Health

Prolonged gaming sessions can result in physical strain and discomfort if not managed carefully. Several players get so engaged in the game that they forget to take care of their body, leading to aches and pains. To negate these outcomes, consider following these healthful practices.

- **Regular Breaks**

A sedentary lifestyle is a doorway to numerous health issues, including obesity, diabetes, cardiovascular diseases, and even cancer. A healthy solution is to take breaks every hour. Stretch, walk around, or do a quick exercise during these intervals.

- **Ergonomic Setup**

Invest in ergonomic gaming equipment such as chairs, keyboards, and mouse pads with wrist support to maintain good posture and prevent musculoskeletal problems. Ensure that your screen is at eye level, and the keyboard and mouse are within an easy, comfortable reach.

- **Hydration and Nutrition**

Staying adequately hydrated and well-nourished is crucial for mental sharpness and physical energy. Keep water and healthy snacks handy during your gaming sessions.

8.2. Mental Well-being

Gaming can be an emotional rollercoaster, triggering elevated bursts of adrenaline, callousness, and even temporary frustration or despair. Players can easily become lost in this torrent of emotions, leading to stress and anxiety. Here are a few tips for maintaining our mental well-being while gaming.

- **Awareness of Emotions**

Recognizing and accepting our gaming-induced emotions is the first step toward controlling them. When you know that stress or anger is creeping in, take a step back and realize it's just a game. You wouldn't want your leisure activity to become your stress trigger.

- **Mindful Gaming**

Reserve time for mindful gaming - where you play not to win, but to enjoy the process, the graphics, the strategy, and the camaraderie with fellow players. Such sessions can be an excellent form of digital detox.

- **Positive Social Interactions**

Online games offer an excellent platform for social interactions. Ensuring these are always positive goes a long way toward a healthier gaming lifestyle. Avoid toxic players, build friendly relations with others, and remember that every player - ally or enemy - is a human too.

8.3. Workout for the Gamer Body

A custom workout plan centered around the muscles most used during gaming can be very beneficial. Stiff neck, sore wrists, and strained shoulders are common among gamers. Here's a routine specifically for gamers:

- **Neck Rolls** - 10 times each in clockwise and anti-clockwise direction
- **Wrist rotations** - 20 times each in both directions
- **Shoulder Rolls** - 10 times forward and backward
- **Cardio training** - short bursts of high-intensity workout
- **Strength training** - focusing on the back, arms, and neck muscles

This routine should ideally be performed every alternate day to provide ample recovery time.

8.4. Mindful Pause: In-game and Out-game

Utilizing pause points within games can serve as opportunities to check in with our body and mind. Similarly, gradually transitioning from game-world to real-world by taking a few mindful breaths or meditating can prevent the feeling of being abruptly uprooted from the virtual world.

Regularly taking these "mindful pauses" can make the gaming experience more enjoyable and less tense, leading to greater overall satisfaction.

In conclusion, we must remember that gaming should enhance our lives, not deplete us. By cultivating healthy habits, investing in ergonomic gaming tools, paying attention to our mental health, strengthening our bodies, and employing mindful breaks, we can enjoy gaming without compromising our physical and mental well-being. After all, we game to explore, enjoy, and evolve, both in the virtual world and outside it.

Chapter 9. Gaming with a Purpose: Social Impact through Digital Play

Gaming, often viewed as a leisure pursuit, a casual escapade in another world, has begun to be embraced in a completely new light - "Gaming with a Purpose." This forward-thinking approach centers on leveraging the power of gaming to foster social impact. From education to public health to socio-cultural dialogue, the scope of digital games is broadening, making the virtual world a place to form, reform, and inform views and actions in the real world.

9.1. Gaming and Education

In a world where traditional education systems often fail to engage students fully, digital games have emerged as powerful tools to foster interactive learning. They are being used to explain complicated concepts, enhance cognitive abilities, and engage learners in a way that textbooks often can't.

Educational games such as Minecraft: Education Edition have gained widespread acceptance, helping students understand complex concepts in STEM and humanities alike. Similarly, games like Prodigy Math are utilizing the addictive nature of gaming to teach children math. According to a study by LearningWorks for Kids, young gamers exhibited improved memory, focus, and spatial-reasoning skills - all of which are attributes contributing to successful learning.

9.2. Games for Public Health

Public health is another domain where games have been instrumental in raising awareness and effecting behavior change. In

2014, the World Health Organization collaborated with game developers to create "The Mission: Immuno," a game aimed at educating public about pandemic outbreaks like Ebola. This game, available in six languages, has been effective in raising awareness and guiding health policies in susceptible regions.

Recently, the game Plague Inc. was lauded for educating its players about the spread of diseases and the importance of preventative measures. These games, packaged with immersive and exciting gameplay, are fostering healthier societies one player at a time.

9.3. Games for Cross-Cultural Understanding

In a culturally diverse world, bridging gaps in understanding is essential for peaceful coexistence. Empathy-focused games such as 'That Dragon, Cancer' and 'Papo & Yo' have allowed players to experience situations that they might otherwise never encounter, helping foster respect and empathy for others' experiences.

Virtual reality games add another layer to this experience. Consider the UN's VR-based game, 'Clouds Over Sidra', that allows us to live in a Syrian refugee camp. This powerfully immersive experience promotes empathy and understanding better than any news article or documentary could.

9.4. Social Issues through Gaming

Ideological polarization is one of the significant challenges of our time. Through narrative-driven and ethical dilemma based games, designers can elicit thought and conversation concerning divisive topics. For example, 'Life Is Strange,' a game that explores issues around mental health, peer pressure, and the socio-economic divide, has created a safe space to discuss these sensitive issues among its players.

Games can also prompt players to think about environmental conservation. 'Endangered', a game about saving species from extinction, empowers players to tackle challenging environmental issues. This game has sparked dialogue about conservation among its player base, inspiring real-world action.

9.5. Games for Emotional Well-being

In recent years, the importance of mental health has taken center stage. Games designed to promote emotional well-being are on the rise. Titles such as 'Kind Words (Lo-Fi Chill Beats to Write To)' provide a platform for players to reach out for emotional support or offer encouragement to others. 'Journey', another popular game, is designed to evoke powerful emotional responses, leading players on a journey of self-discovery and reflection.

The rise of the 'empathy game' genre proves that games have moved beyond being mere sources of entertainment. They have become means to understand and express what it means to be human and connected.

9.6. Conclusion

The virtual world of gaming is no longer an escape from reality but a mirror reflecting our collective humanity. The joy and camaraderie, the empathy and understanding, the willingness to learn, and the inspiration for change - all are proof of the power and potential of gaming for social impact. Yes, the digital rain may be heavy, but it waters seeds of growth and enlightenment. In this gaming landscape, we don't merely play - we engage, learn, empathize, act, and grow.

However, it's essential to recognize the potential pitfalls of gaming, such as addiction, isolation, and violence. By staying aware and committed to balance, we can turn the fields of the digital realm into fertile ground for both fun and furtherance. As we navigate this digital downpour, we're not just gamers; we're proactive participants molding the virtual into the real. We are, indeed, gaming with a purpose. Thus, an adherent approach towards 'The Mindful Gamer's Guide' ensures that we play responsibly and purposefully in this digital downpour.

Chapter 10. The Future Awaits: Potential Developments in the Gaming Sphere

In the wake of the digital revolution, the realm of video gaming has become a major player in entertainment and social networking. As technology advances at a dizzying pace, we stand at the precipice of an entirely new era in gaming.

10.1. Advancements in Virtual Reality

Virtual Reality (VR) has been a focal point of innovation for many years. Though VR systems, such as the Oculus Rift or Vive, have already seen a good deal of success, the technology is in its infancy and has a long way to go. Currently, VR developers face a host of challenges, from preventing simulation sickness to designing intuitive controls. However, as VR gear continues to improve, the quality of VR games is also expected to rise significantly.

Furthermore, current VR technologies are mainly used for visual and auditory stimulation. But as they advance, we can expect other senses to become more engaged. Some researchers are exploring ways to simulate touch and movement, creating truly immersive environments. This could heighten the sense of presence in the virtual world, making games more engaging and realistic.

10.2. Rise of Cloud Gaming

The recent emergence of cloud gaming platforms, like Google's Stadia or Microsoft's xCloud, is set to redefine our gaming experiences. With cloud gaming, the raw computing power of your machine is irrelevant, as games are streamed over the internet, similar to how we stream movies on Netflix or Amazon Prime.

As the internet becomes faster and more accessible, cloud gaming could democratize access to high-definition gaming, making it available regardless of the specifications of your device or your geographical location. Additionally, it could potentially end the era of physical disks or downloads, making room for a future where we rent games as a service.

10.3. Augmentation through AI

Artificial Intelligence (AI) is another powerful force impacting the landscape of digital gaming. AI is already used in games to power non-player characters (NPCs) and game physics. But its role could become much more significant. Future games may use AI to dynamically adapt to a player's behavior and preferences, altering environments, storylines, and challenges in real-time.

AI might also revolutionize online multiplayer games by creating intelligent bots that can match or even surpass human performance. This could introduce new layers of competition and cooperation and offer players the chance to interact with AI characters that feel as real as human counterparts.

10.4. Immersive Storytelling

Storytelling methods in games have evolved immensely, from text-based narratives to voice-acted cutscenes. Yet, the future holds more advancements for narrative-driven games. In particular, developers will continually refine how games respond to players' decisions, making stories more flexible and adaptable.

Games of the future might offer narrative arcs that genuinely evolve based on player actions, decisions, and characters' development. This could elevate games from simple storytelling platforms to genuinely collaborative narrative design spaces.

10.5. Technological Innovations: Beyond Gaming

It's important to recognize that advancements in gaming technology often spill over into other fields. Developments in virtual reality are being used not only for gaming but also in medicine, aiding in physical therapy and mental health treatment. AI advancements in gaming can influence other sectors, such as robotic technology and self-driving cars.

Cloud computing, another technology essential to future gaming, also contributes to fields such as scientific research and environmental modeling. As the gaming industry continues to innovate, we can expect these technologies to have ripple effects far beyond gaming.

10.6. Navigating the Technological Shift: A Call to Mindful Gaming

Even as technology continually reshapes the gaming landscape, it's essential for us as gamers to remain mindful. The changes we've touched upon present exciting opportunities. However, they also raise questions about our relationships with games, technology, and each other.

The potentially limitless immersion offered by VR, the adaptability of AI, and the accessibility of cloud gaming all promise profound changes in how we play and what we play. They also challenge us to maintain a healthy balance between immersion and reality. These technologies draw us into their worlds, but let's remember, they're there for our enjoyment. We shouldn't be swept away by the digital downpour, but learn how to dance in it. As mindful gamers, we can navigate this vast digital realm with intention and purpose, playing not just to win, but to learn, grow, and connect.

Chapter 11. Your Interactive Guide: Sailing Through the Storm To Mastery

Just as a sailor, braving the unpredictable seas armed with a seasoned captain's astuteness, reliance on innovative technology, and the sheer will to conquer the challenges, the journey of a gamer is no different. Our endeavour in the following treatise is to guide you, as you navigate through this stormy sea of digital games, to prosper into a mentally agile, strategic, and most importantly, a mindful player.

11.1. The Rudder and the Compass: Choosing Your Conflict and Navigating it

The vast gaming ocean provides you with an immense diversity of games—from serene puzzle games serving the subtlest intellectual satiety to high-paced, strategy-driven MOBA games for a thrill-seeker's delight. One must, before stepping forth, understand the nature of the game, the conflict it offers - and navigate through it mindfully.

With genres, comes the variety of conflicts – man vs man, man vs self, man vs society, or man vs nature. Every genre offers unique encounters and challenges, and understanding the nature of one's game is the first step in forming a strategy. Try to identify the narrative, the intents of the characters (yours, and those around you), the mechanics they adopt, and the goals they strive for.

Every game has a locus. Some may offer an extensive open-world experience, like 'The Witcher 3' and 'Red Dead Redemption 2', some offer smaller but no less complex worlds like 'Among Us'. You, the protagonist or team, traverse in these worlds carrying an objective, endowed with a set of abilities, perhaps shared or unique, to achieve those objectives. Understanding these nuances, using the conflict and settings to your advantage, and planning your approach accordingly is pivotal to set a strong sail.

11.2. Setting Sail: Building An Effective Strategy

Equipped with the knowledge of your conflict, the sailing can truly begin. The sea you are in is not a peaceful estuary but a tornado-stricken ocean. Success in gaming needs a fool-proof strategy, the ability to foresee possible complications, and the readiness to deal with unseen obstacles.

Consider strategy games like 'Chess' or 'StarCraft 2', the outcome depends intensely upon the players' strategy. Foreseeing opponent moves, countering them, planning your resources, and making definitive strikes; it's a mind game encapsulating diligence and dexterity. Even with shooters like 'Call of Duty', understanding the map, planning an ambush or evasive manoeuvres can swing the opportunities in your favour.

It's critical to steep deeply into the meta-game, understanding the rock-paper-scissors mechanics most games would follow. Studying your opponents, predicting their moves, strategising every single step, every single resource could be the difference between winning or losing a game, and can serve as a powerful booster to your overall gaming performance.

11.3. The Eye of the Storm: Ensuring Psychological Well-being

Engulfed in this ever-evolving digital downpour, continuously battling the seething currents, maintaining psychological well-being becomes paramount. Understandably, gaming can be intense. However, games are supposed to be a source of joy and relaxation, not stress and anxiety.

It is essential to keep track of one's mental well-being. Do not let a loss or a win define you. A game is an ensemble of numerous variables, and an outer expression of your inner state. A bad day doesn't tag you as a bad player. Break ties with toxic gamers who steal your joy and confidence.

Many games these days include mechanics to ensure psychological health, like Nintendo Switch's friendly reminder to take breaks. Acknowledging such prompts and actively implementing them helps maintain a balance between gaming and life beyond it.

11.4. Weathering the Storm: Practical Tips and Tricks

Just as squalls pass, it's essential to remember that the phase of struggling in a game passes too. Consider these tips:

1. Using Tutorials and Training modes: These are designed to usher you into the mechanics of the game, use them wisely. Even experienced players return to these modes to sharpen their skills or try out new strategies.

2. Research: Use online forums, watch experienced streamers or pros play, learn the best practices and apply them to your game.

3. Keep experimenting: Don't constrain yourself to one gameplay

style or character role. Experiment with different styles, characters, roles, it not only adds versatility to your game but also makes you unpredictable.

4. Breaks: Long gaming sessions can impact your performance, take regular breaks to rejuvenate.

5. Practice : "Practice makes a man perfect," they say. Play regularly, understand your improvement areas, and focus more on them.

With careful selection of your gaming path, conscientious strategy construction, mindful attunement and a healthy, respectful state of mind towards yourself and others, sailing through the storm to the shores of mastery is not a far cry.

In the end, gaming boils down to an experience of joy and self-improvement, making you more nimble, strategic and adaptive, traits useful not just in the game, but also in life. Therefore, as you venture forth into diverse digital realms, remember, the purpose is not just to conquer the game, but through its lens, to conquer oneself, and in the process, to savour the journey too.

www.ingramcontent.com/pod-product-compliance
Lightning Source LLC
Chambersburg PA
CBHW061056050326
40690CB00012B/2642